MERCEDES ~BENZ

SL & SLC

Osprey AutoHistory

MERCEDES ~BENZ
SL & SLC

L J K SETRIGHT

First published in 1979 by Osprey Publishing Limited,
27A Floral Street, London WC2E 9DP
Member company of the George Philip Group

This revised edition published in 1986

United States Distribution by

Osceola, Wisconsin 54020, USA

British Library Cataloguing in Publication Data

Setright, L.J.K.
    Mercedes-Benz roadsters.—2nd ed—
    (Osprey AutoHistory)
    1. Mercedes automobile—History
    I. Title
    629.2'222   TL215.M4
ISBN 0–85045–698–3

Filmset and printed in England by
BAS Printers Limited, Over Wallop, Hampshire

Contents

CHAPTER 1

Antecedents
and Uhlenhaut

Nobility is a quality that is not easily attained in the motor industry. Inheritance of it is possible, but the history of the industry is not so long that we could forget how such a distinction was originally earned. In the case of Mercedes-Benz, whose right to a place in the highest rank of car manufacturers must be undisputed, the testimony of the past is supported by evidence of the present, for they continue to wage the double campaign that they have fought since their earliest times—on the one front, to be in the vanguard of scientific and technological progress, on the other to fight a rearguard battle against the social and commercial temptations that have introduced the mean and the compromising to corrupt the standards of other manufacturers. For a hundred years they have pursued these ideals, and nobody could have done it longer: the proprietors of Mercedes-Benz are the company Daimler-Benz AG, an amalgamation of the two firms that created the motor car and the industry that eventually grew up around it.

It was at the end of June 1926 that Benz & Cie and the Daimler Motoren Gesellschaft entered into an association of common interest and ultimately complete amalgamation in the constitution of the new Daimler-Benz company. Already, both firms had enjoyed the services of outstanding engineers: Gottlieb Daimler had been assisted by the visionary Wilhelm Maybach, whose outstanding new designs which appeared in 1901 had set the morphological pattern for the development of the modern motor car, and he was followed in 1907 by the founder's son, Paul Daimler, as Chief Engineer and Designer. When Paul vacated the post in 1922 it was taken by no less historical a figure than Dr. Ferdinand Porsche, who like his predecessor came to Daimler after spending some time at Austro-Daimler. As for that other pioneer, Karl Benz, he enjoyed the services of Dr. Hans Niebel, who assumed the technical direction of the Mercedes-Benz programme after the amalgamation, assisted by another Benz inheritance in the form of Wagner, who had been directly concerned with racing cars at Benz, thus sharing a professional interest with the others.

The influence of motor racing on motor car design and manufacture is not to be denied. Even if it does not always produce hardware for assimilation into the production cars of the manufacturer concerned (a study of Mercedes-Benz history will produce examples to show that in some cases it is the touring car of today that is the racing car of tomorrow, in direct opposition to the sequence of the popular adage), there is no questioning the importance of the standards that a familiarity with motor racing gives to the designer of a touring car. To compete is to discover what is possible; and few creative people, be they musical composers or motor car designers, will be content to exploit less than what they know to be possible. Thus the touring car inherits from the racing car, usually at some distance in time, the standards of steering, road holding and braking, handling and general controllability, as well perhaps though not necessarily of sheer acceleration and speed, with which we identify much that is taken to represent progress in car engineering.

There is more to progress than going faster or even stopping faster. The other half is more a matter of physical welfare than of sensual satisfaction, embracing matters of comfort, convenience, durability, economy and, in the most narrow-minded sense, respectability.

Successfully to combine both these kinds of evolution, to satisfy at once the criteria both of the market place and of the race track, is to achieve a further degree of civilisation of the car.

It is difficult to define that word *civilization*, but the art historian Sir Kenneth Clark made a valiant attempt: "Civilization means something more than energy and will and creative power. . . . How can I define it? Well, very shortly a sense of permanence." Hope for the future is implicit in that wonderful definition, hope for a better future being surely of the very essence of our ambition for civilization. One does not civilize a sword by blunting its edge but by converting it into a ploughshare. Similarly with cars, it is not good enough that conflicting requirements (as of ride comfort and roadholding, for example) should be allowed to compromise each other; properly, they should be made complementary to each other. When that is done successfully, the result may be a sports car.

Throughout the joint and several histories of Mercedes and Benz, there have been sports cars. The blend of track and town, iron fist and velvet glove has not always been as smooth as might be hoped; there was too much sports in some of them, too much car in others.

In turn the most brilliant and most baffling of them all, the most lumpen blend of *suaviter in modo* and *fortiter in re*, was the 300 SL. The practical proof of this car had been in the sports car races of 1952—none of the mean and trifling ones, just the important events such as the 24-hour Le Mans race, the Carrera Panamericana Mexico and the sports car Grands Prix of Switzerland and Germany, all of which it won. Everyone raved about its streamlined two-seater body with the gull-wing doors, recognizing at once how they promised ease of entry and exit in a narrow garage or parking slot or the means of a glamourous arrival at some gathering of the élite—and only reflecting later on the accompanying threat of disaster in a roll-over accident. Everyone raved about the prodigious power and extraordinary flexibility given to the inclined six-cylinder engine (from the Type 300 saloon) by direct fuel injection into the cylinders. The speed of the car shook the Jaguar team rigid when they met in the Mille Miglia; but there was even more than that to the 300 SL. It had the first true spaceframe chassis, a properly triangulated structure of small-diameter steel tubes subjected only to axial loads and giving the car a foundation of exceptional lightness and rigidity. It was a spaceframe that was much the more complex and somewhat the more perfect of the two that pioneered the idea in 1952, the other car being Colin Chapman's Lotus 6, which was no more a production car than the early factory racer 300 SL. By 1954, the 300 SL was in production and on the market, tamed and trimmed for touring; and it was a good year for marketing a sports car, being that in which Mercedes-Benz returned to the top of the motor racing tree, where it had been undisputed champion fifteen years earlier. The effect was as shattering as it had been in 1934, when the return

Uhlenhaut: butter would not melt in his boot

of Mercedes-Benz to grand prix racing had defined the start of a new era in racing car engineering, and engineer Uhlenhaut, who had been so intimately concerned with the development of those furiously powerful, curiously portentous pre-war cars, now excelled himself in the development of a new car for the new 1954 racing formula, embodying all that experience had shown valuable and more that advanced technology showed desirable. There can never have been a first-class racing car so rich in innovations and heterodoxies as the $2\frac{1}{2}$-litre unsupercharged W196 Mercedes-Benz, nor ever such a car so successful. It bore little superficial relationship to the great racing cars that had preceded it, whether from Mercedes-Benz or elsewhere, and its success therefore might be seen as confirming the value of the original thinking that it represented.

The fact that the W196 did not go as fast as might have been expected may be partly explained by the lack of really effective competition at the time that it was current; but it is also known that the car had originally been intended to enjoy a longer competitive life than was eventually dictated by circumstance, being designed with a view to progressive development over a span of four years at the end of which it was intended to deploy 400 bhp through all four wheels. The car pioneered a large number of features that were to pass out of currency when it was withdrawn, only to be adopted afresh by other racing car constructors later. While some Mercedes-Benz traditions were sustained, such as the welded fabrication of the engine cylinders and heads and, indeed, the elegant old straight-eight configuration, other traditions which Mercedes-Benz had established, such as the use of the De Dion rear axle, Mercedes-Benz now dismissed. Ironically the accident that prompted the premature

11

The pagoda roof was the outstanding styling feature of the SL series; this is a 280

withdrawal of Daimler-Benz from racing was one that involved a sports car version, the W196/110, with a cast-block 3-litre engine and even more brilliant novelties, including the provision of a large air brake that was extremely effective (and, of course, fade-free) at very high speeds and could be exploited by an intelligent driver (Moss was the only one to do it, to his own and to the joy of its designer) to modify the car's behaviour through corners.

The designer who was responsible for all this, and thereafter devoted the remainder of his most distinguished career to the development—it would not be unreasonable to call it the perfection— of the Mercedes-Benz passenger car was Rudolf Uhlenhaut. When he joined Daimler-Benz, Niebel had not long to live; after all, he had been with Benz before the amalgamation of 1926

With the lid off, the SL was a superbly proportioned open two-seater; this is a 230

and his contribution as first Technical Director of Daimler-Benz was in setting the high standards for which Mercedes-Benz engineering became famous. Sound in talent and training, Uhlenhaut rose from being racing service manager to the office of Chief Designer as Niebel's post-war successor.

He must have seemed little more than a clever and cultivated lad when he first joined Daimler-Benz AG, a mannerly young man in his very early twenties, born in Germany, brought up in England and educated in both. It was not long before he was chosen to take charge of the new Racing Service Division being formed to develop and field the fantastic new cars built for the 750 kilogram grand prix formula of 1933–37. His reaction was typical: confident that he had all the necessary theoretical knowledge, he embarked on a training

13

programme through which he might acquire the necessary practical knowledge. He wanted to recognize the problems that his drivers would have to face but which they might not be able to recount in terms satisfactory to the engineer.

So he got hold of a racing car and drove it, round and round the Nurburgring, starting at a pace such as he might run with an ordinary touring car and rapidly increasing it until he satisfied himself that he was virtually as fast as the best professional racing drivers. He always insisted that driving a racing car was no different in essentials from driving a touring car, and the results that he achieved commanded respect for that view. He himself commanded four engineers and fifty mechanics in direct charge of ten complete cars with another ten spare engines, and he could call if necessary on the services of another 220 first-class fitters at the factory, where the drawing office and works were responsible for the design and production of the cars. In those days, when political and commercial preferment were tendered by the newly successful National Socialist Government to those car and motor-cycle manufacturers who would demonstrate internationally the supposedly innate superiority of the Germans in everything they did, Daimler-Benz spent annually on racing a sum that by 1986 values might be equated to about 3 million pounds Sterling. During the last three years of racing before Germany became involved in more mortal conflicts, seasons in which the Mercedes-Benz team was overwhelmingly successful, it must have been evident to the directors of Daimler-Benz AG that the small portion of this colossal investment that showed the best return was Uhlenhaut's salary.

At the end of the World War, a new start had to be made, for according to a statement issued by

Pre-production model of the 105 bhp 190 SL of 1954

the Directors in 1945, Daimler-Benz had ceased to exist. Three-quarters of their plant had been destroyed, communications were non-existent, disruption and devastation complete. Yet people and things were gradually brought together again and Uhlenhaut was appointed to take complete charge of car designs and development. He held this position until his retirement in the early 1970s and throughout that period his work reflected every facet of his incomparably impressive personality. He was a charming man, courteous and completely approachable and ready to talk with anybody; he was blessed with a formidable intellect, giving him complete command of the science and technologies that were his stock-in-trade. Punctilious in every detail, he epitomized the thoroughness that we recognize as a German tradition. Finally, and not least relevant to the subject of this book, he was insistent in applying to his cars the exacting standards of a driver who was capable of lapping the Nurburgring in a W196 at an average speed within two per cent of that achieved in the same car by that greatest of drivers Juan-Manuel Fangio. One thing about him that was particularly nice was that he did not allow his proficiency in theory to obscure simple issues: his standard test for thermal insulation of a luggage boot was to put a kilo of butter in it and settle for a hard day's drive into the mountains, at the end of which the butter should not have melted.

The reputation earned in the last third of a century by Mercedes-Benz cars, for quality, performance, roadworthiness and safety, owes more to this polite colossus than to anyone else. It is a reputation that might be summed up in the word *integrity*. When the time came (or was perhaps a little overdue early in the 1960s) to replace the viciously powerful 300 SL and its vapidly pretentious sibling the 190 SL, the car that Uhlenhaut put in their place was one of the most beautifully integrated that Daimler-Benz or anybody else had ever produced.

CHAPTER 2

Swing-axle
Light-weight

There was nothing new in the confusion that reigned in 1963 about how to define or for that matter to recognize a sports car. Early English Perpendicular notions (a sports car is one into which it is impossible to enter without either stooping or removing one's hat) and late American Horizontal (a sports car is one in which the front seats fold down to form beds) had been dismissed as insufficient, while objectively practical suggestions such as that of the late L. E. W. Pomeroy (a sports car is one which prompts its driver to handle it in sporting fashion) were too vague in the scope they left for the imagination of the unfledged and the cynicism of the experienced. There was also a general tendency, becoming particularly evident in the early 1960s, for sports cars to be supposed cheap and impractical versions of stodgy family saloons produced by cutting off the roof and shortening the wheelbase. All over the world it became common practice for major manufacturers to exploit their parts shelves by putting the most surprisingly mundane bits into the most unjustifiably expensive sporting machinery. This could be observed on every scale from the minute MG Midget to the monstrous

Ford Mustang, and in almost all cases the humble origins of such cars were betrayed by a humiliating inability to match the comportment (however much they might match the speed) of better-bred sports cars made by competition-oriented specialists. Nevertheless this trend encouraged, and was encouraged by, the multitude of customers and critics who by this time were at least agreed that sports cars had progressed from the days when they were cramped, uncomfortable and devoid of weather protection or any amenities. The modern idea had become that the sports car was a fully equipped sophisticated vehicle, de-

Low, wide, and handsome, SL proportions were an assurance of good stability

signed for covering long distances at reasonably high speeds in all kinds of climates and having ample accommodation for the luggage of two people with expensive tastes. Thirty years earlier, perhaps even only fifteen years earlier, when a sports car was still a noisy and draughty agglomeration of RSJs and flying buttresses, such a vehicle would have been categorized as a GT—*gran turismo, voiture de grand tourisme* or even, if you insisted long and hard enough, a car in which to undertake the Grand Tour. Mercedes-Benz did not mind unduly: they were content to describe their new 230 SL as a sports car.

Large glazed areas gave excellent vision from within the coupé top

A few of the press critics who saw it make its debut at the Geneva Motor Show in March 1963 challenged this description. They were diehards who doubtless felt it necessary to prove themselves such by being a bit sniffy about the elegant little Mercedes, which was not as fast as the mighty 300 SL and, dash it, could be bought with automatic transmission and power steering! Everyone else, including most notably the pressmen who had already driven it, was quite content with the car's popular appellation. Did not the use by Mercedes-Benz of the suffix SL constitute sufficient guarantee?

According to the Stuttgart code, the letter S might stand for either Sport or Super, and the L stood for Leicht (meaning light in weight) more often than it stood for Luxus (which, of course, stands for everything imaginable and nothing that can hurt). Any and all of these terms would be fair when applied to the new 230 two-seater; whatever people thought, it was a sports car.

In fact, the specification for the 230 SL actually started with cornering power, and the rest of the design extended from that premise. The 300 SL may have been shockingly fast in a straight line, but the deficiences of its rear suspension geometry, with two swinging half-axles producing a most undesirable variation in wheel camber and roll-centre height as the suspension was deflected, forced the driver to rely and indeed to tread heavily on his brakes before negotiating a corner. One might come out fast but only if one went in slowly, and any attempt to be more enterprising would lead only to sudden and incorrigible unstable oversteer. As for the mechanically more humdrum 190 SL, the lower-priced roadster that had so little in common with the 300 SL apart from the general styling of its bodywork, the poor thing was scarcely powerful enough or fast enough to

Too much brightwork and not enough legibility

get itself into any kind of trouble anyway, and might comfortably be dismissed from any consideration of what a sports car ought to be able to do. What Uhlenhaut expected of a sports car was that it should reflect the experience and progress gained and made in recent racing car engineering; in other words, it should accept the standards that racing can always be expected to set. The 1960s was a period in which the contemporary grand prix racing car had a chassis that was, so to speak, faster than the engine, and so long as it were fast enough, a sports car fashioned with similar priorities ought to be unexceptionable in almost any market. What was wanted was that both the

Distributor and injection pump drives had a common source in the sweet 230 SL engine

300 and 190 SL models should be replaced by one car that was as much as possible a combination of those two, a comfortable two-seater that was neither too big nor too expensive, one that was fast enough to be exhilarating and perhaps even exciting but not necessarily so fast as to be frightening—but above all, one that was beautifully sprung for a comfortable ride and yet sensational in corners. Back in the days around

1931 when Uhlenhaut had started work with Daimler-Benz as a technical assistant in the carburation department, the Englishman Maurice Olley had been starting the modern science of roadholding and handling in the experimental workshops of General Motors; and by the mid-1950s Uhlenhaut knew, not only from studying the theories first propounded by Olley but also from practical experience, that with properly competent engineering whatever is done to improve roadholding ought also to improve ride qualities. It was not an impossibility that he sought, therefore, but something that demanded no more than his own professional expertise and some glutinous modern tyres that would provide the kind of cushioned grip that he sought.

As installed, the engine's air manifold without carburettors was the most unusual feature

Nowadays, one would simply specify the latest in low-profile radial tyres and take it for granted that they would be more than satisfactory. In those days when the 230 SL was being confected, there were already radial ply tyres available, but they were not yet commonplace and they left a good deal to be desired. Already they were recognized as offering higher cornering power, better braking, better traction and a quieter, more comfortable high-speed ride than contemporary bias-ply tyres; on the other hand they also condemned the car to a harsher low-speed ride, to an uncomfortably sudden loss of grip and final break-away when the limits of their cornering power were transgressed, and to an inconsistently variable rate of response to steering inputs. Accordingly Daimler-Benz asked two German tyre manufacturers, Continental and Firestone-Phoenix, to create special tyres for the embryo 230 SL, asking for wide section, generous treads, scuff protection ribbing projecting out of the exterior side walls (making the tyres asymmetric) and a whole host of dynamic requirements in which good steering response ranked high.

What they got was a tyre that Continental christened the Halbgürtel, which means literally half-belted—a curious misnomer, for this braced-tread tyre had four circumferential belts of rayon cords beneath its tread. What actually made it a half-way (some might have said half-baked) affair was that the body plies were not truly radial, as was normally the case in a belted tyre. The idea was to improve sidewall stiffness, which had been the subject of concentrated study and was to remain so for several more years, in the effort to improve the handling characteristics of radial-ply tyres in the more violent type of manoeuvres. It was some time before designers learned the importance of controlling the flexibility of the sidewalls in tyres of this type, as this flexibility permitted an appreciable delay in response between tyre tread and wheel rim. This delay is cumulative from one end of the car to the other in all steering manoeuvres, and stimulates yaw instability. Furthermore, radial-ply side walls are especially sensitive to the transmission of tractive or braking torques which, according to circumstances, might degrade or heighten their lateral response. Accordingly the tyre manufacturers searched for ways of increasing the

Well-arranged pedals, gearlever and everything correctly placed: a driver's car

*First Continental radial-ply
SL tyre, the RA60*

real or apparent stiffness of the sidewalls to improve lateral response; they did not want to reduce the flexural ability of the sidewalls, for it was this that provided the cushioning and accommodated variations in the distance between tread and wheel rim, but they did want to avoid the distortion that permitted lateral displacement of the tread with respect to the rim. It was found that this side wall compliance or capacity for lateral distortion could be reduced by tilting the cords slightly from the truly radial disposition, in which they crossed the equatorial or centre-line of the tread at 90°, and both Continental and Firestone decided to make it a significant tilt, angling the carcass cords at 80° or even 70°. Because of the dimensional incorruptibility of the breaker belts, this angling of the normally radial cords preloaded the sidewalls in such a way as to reduce their sensitivity to tractive or braking torques and to tauten their response to lateral displacement as in steering. These tyres were tantamount to belted bias-ply tyres, which were not in themselves a new concept at all: in the early 1950s Dunlop had built tyres of the same nature for use by the Jaguars at Le Mans. Certainly the lateral response was good, possibly the crispest of anything outside racing, and the cornering power (a very different matter) could be surprisingly high too: but it was notable that the rolling resistance of the belted-bias tyre, gratifyingly low up to about 90 mph (145 km/h), rose steeply beyond. This sharp increase in consumption was evidence of distressing internal tensions, for the carcase at high speeds would suffer excessive shear loadings in the shoulders beneath the treads, where breaker and body plies were pulling in different ways, severely aggravating the possibility of fatigue failure.

The discovery of these shortcomings lay in the

future. With the specially commissioned new tyres looking promising, Uhlenhaut next began to look for suspension that would allow them to be exploited. For years Mercedes-Benz had been committed to swing-axle rear geometry, but the faster the car the more besetting the technical problems. The grand prix cars of the mid-1930s had shown this eloquently enough, but if any further proof were needed the 300 SL had recently supplied it. On the other hand the sophisticated solutions followed in the rear suspension of the W196 Grand Prix car had demonstrated that if the radius of gyration of the half-axles were great enough and the roll centre low enough, then the car might be made to behave very well indeed. As first applied to passenger cars, the Stuttgart solution was to divide the rear axle in such a way as would give it a single central pivot set low underneath the differential casing, which was made integral with one half of the axle: the roll centre was thus brought commensurately low, and if the track were then widened enough for the

For a customer who wanted to know which 230 SL in the car-park was his, this special body was built by Pininfarina

27

Eugen Böhringer and Klaus Kaiser in the 1964 Spa-Sofia-Liège rally finished with their 230 SL hurt by a sheep

angles of deviation of the two axle halves to be reduced to a tolerable minimum even when the suspension was at full deflection, then the terrifying consequences of violent camber change or jacking-up of the tail of the car might be avoided. A later refinement was the addition of a transverse compensator spring (at first a helical coil, and later still a pneumatic cylinder) working through levers over the differential to apply additional springing in the bump condition (equivalent to progressive-rate springing to countervail the carriage of heavy loads in the luggage boot) without affecting the spring rates in the roll condition when cornering. All this theory was applied to the design of the 230 SL, which also accepted as a matter of course the double wishbone front suspension already fitted to the then current 190, 220 and 300 saloons. Thus the front and rear tracks were the same as in the saloons, a notably generous measure of 58·5 inches (1486 mm); but the wheelbase at 94 inches (2400 mm) was more than 14 inches (350 mm) shorter than that of the saloons and coupés in the 220 and 300 range; and although this might be expected to increase the car's susceptibility to pitch changes in braking and accelerating, it would also make it more lively in answering the helm.

The engine, too, would have to be derived from current production, but the design brief expressed or implied some scope to modify or develop it somewhat. The choice of the 6-cylinder single overhead camshaft (M127) engine as fitted to the then current 220 SE saloon seemed a foregone conclusion: it was an engine that had been developed from its very beginning as a highly efficient unit, because the company had wanted to endow a big and heavy luxury saloon with a respectable performance and yet avoid intimidating customers with the prospect of having to pay heavy taxes in countries where cars were taxed according to their engine displacements. However, even that 220 SE engine, designed with a short crankshaft running in only four main bearings so that it could run to high speeds without problems of torsional flutter, and furnished with fuel injection to ensure high combustion and thermal efficiencies, was hardly a complete answer to Uhlenhaut's requirements: in its normal SE saloon form it produced only 14

*Böhringer and Kaiser in the
1963 Spa-Sofia-Liège rally,
which they won*

bhp more than the woebegone 4-cylinder 190 SL which preceded it, and it weighed a good deal more despite an aluminium-alloy cylinder block and head. The conventions of tuning to boost its output could easily be applied, however: first its cylinders were increased in bore by 2 mm to amplify the total displacement from 2195 to 2306 cc. Next the compression ratio was raised from 8·7 to 9·3:1. To increase the breathing capacity to match the increased displacement, the valves were enlarged and the exhaust system altered. Finally they changed the Bosch manifold fuel injection system for an alternative Bosch type which squirted directly into the inlet ports.

This last feature bemused quite a number of experts who feared that Daimler-Benz had not reached any final conclusions about how fuel ought to be injected. In the 300 SL sports car engine, as in the M196 Grand Prix engine, the fuel was injected directly into each cylinder from a diesel-like jerk pump having one plunger for each cylinder. In the 220 SE and 300 SE touring cars, there was a 2-cylinder pump driven at engine speed, one plunger feeding three cylinders through a distributor block and the other supplying the other three cylinders similarly; and the injector nozzles were set in the air manifold, which was often held to be responsible for the questionable starting and erratic idling of these cars. For the 230 SL, a six-plunger jerk pump, driven as in the sports and racing cars at half engine speed, supplied injector nozzles planted in the inlet ports, actually in the cylinder head rather than in the manifold.

The first figures issued for the performance of this engine were of the gross type, referring to 170 bhp at 5600 rpm and 159 lb/ft of torque (equivalent to a brake mean effective pressure of 171 lb per square inch) at 4500 rpm. Later more realistic and

Böhringer and Kaiser at the Karlsruhe control during the 1963 Marathon

more nearly net figures were adduced: the power output of the engine as installed in the car came to be 150 bhp at 5500 rpm, and the torque of 144 lb/ft would have been equivalent to a BMEP of 155 lb per square inch, which was still excellent by the standards of production cars in those days and would be considered exceptional today.

It was really a very good engine, very efficient and very well made. Evidence in support of this latter contention could be found in the very high mileages that this and indeed all other Mercedes-Benz petrol engines commonly attain. In most cases where a diesel engine can be fitted to a car in place of a petrol engine, the diesel is found to last very much longer because, so apallingly high are

Coming or going, the 250 SL did not noticeably differ from the 230 SL

the internal stresses to which it masochistically subjects itself, if it were not supremely well-made it would tear itself to scrap in next to no time. Petrol engines are seldom constructed with such punctilio, for there is seldom any demand for it and even less frequently is there a customer prepared to pay for it, but the buyer of a Mercedes-Benz car expects and is required to pay for the sort of quality that Dr. Niebel would have insisted on, and so since the petrol engines were as well-made as the diesels, the petrol engines lasted as long.

Given such a splendid propellant, it remained for the car to be fitted out with other mechanical elements that would be complementary. Some of them could be taken for granted: the clutch and four-speed synchromesh gearbox, like the optional alternative of a fluid coupling and four-speed automatic gearbox, were adopted from the production saloons, and so was the traditional Mercedes-Benz recirculating ball steering with optional servo assistance to help overcome the rather high loads that could be imposed from the special new tyres. In the matter of brakes Uhlenhaut was a little more adventurous: for the rear wheels there remained the familiar drums, with ferrous liners bonded by the Alfin chemical process to light-alloy radial-finned shrouds, but for the front wheels British Girling disc brakes were specified (the first time that discs were used in a Mercedes-Benz car of any kind) with a Master Vac servo built into the circuit.

All these components were buttoned into a pressed steel chassis pan designed to act as the integrated floor platform of a similarly constructed body. The multi-tubular spaceframe chassis and aluminium panelling of the 300 SL had been more or less a *jeu d'esprit*; Daimler-Benz had abandoned the wicked old ways of separate chassis and espoused the more appealing cause of a stressed-skin hull back in 1953, when their big-volume models were also blessed with the single pivot rear axle; and nothing was likely to make them revert to their old practises again.

Over and above all this was the stunningly handsome body, which attracted far more admiration than the car's technical specification when it first appeared at the Geneva Show—and for that matter still does. Its contours were simple and squat but they were exciting, with proportions that emphasized the tremendously wide track and low-slung mass. It looked crisp and athletically trim, something that we were not accustomed to in Mercedes-Benz. None of the other cars in the range were anywhere near as

Hard cornering caused little roll, but already the negative camber of the rear wheel can be seen

inspiring: they might enjoy all the same essential virtues but they could not be enjoyed, for their superstructure was always drawn with too heavy a hand. It was not just a matter of carrying so much garish brightwork, for the SL was by no means short of it; it was simply that everything, even to the details of trim and upholstery and in-strumentation, was wrought on too massive a scale. Everything in the other Mercs not only appeared too big, it actually was too big. The saloons seemed indeed to have been designed for

Did those tyres' kerbing ribs affect spray patterns?

Why does the owner of such a car want to advertise its automatic transmission?

drivers who were fairly tall and very fat: it ought to have limited their market considerably, as well as confining it even further in certain countries where in those days a Mercedes-Benz saloon was not considered a car for a gentleman; but Daimler-Benz were presumably not worried, for they sold quantities to people who were, to judge from the way they drove, by no means gentle folk. The SL was different: here at last was a sports car that a gentleman would not mind being seen in, nor a lady neither. Here at last was a sporting two-seater that was capable of being anything from a delightful runabout to a handsome road-hugger that looked capable of dealing with far more power than it had (and felt like it) and yet was capable of undertaking the most serious and demanding journeys without concessions to time, place, weather or the driver's physique.

All this was because as well as being handsome it was a sensible body. There were some people who jibbed at the transverse concavity of the roof, failing to see why it should be so depressed in the middle; in fact it had been raised at the edges, to create higher door openings for ease of entry and exit and higher fenestration for a more complete view of the outside world. It could also be bought as a soft-top roadster, or the two forms could be combined with the aid of a detachable hard top beneath which the soft fabric hood could be furled and tucked conveniently away. There would still be plenty of space behind the seats, especially if the customer did not specify the optional transverse seat for a third passenger, who might sit sideways on the right and enjoy the deep footwell on the left. In any case there was a generously big if rather shallow luggage boot in the tail, marred only by the monumental intrusion of the spare wheel—a 185-14 tyre seemed enormous in those days. The broad boot lid made loading easy just as the wide doors made getting in and out far easier than the unsightly scramble dictated by other more spartan sports cars.

Sports cars? Surely this could not be a sports car, what with its pressed steel disc wheels, its elaborate caparisons in baroque chrome, its sumptuous furnishings and Sybaritic fittings? It hardly looked like something that might be master of the open road, more like something given to mollycoddle a mistress. Indeed time was to prove it probably the most perfect of cars in that rôle, an unimpeachable, untemperamental, self-propelled cosmetic aid in which some expensively beautiful lady might take her time down Bond Street, take her pick down Park Avenue, or take her ovation along the Boulevard Haussmann. It is surely one of the greatest possible tributes to the universal competence of Mercedes-Benz that the SL (and this applies to the whole of the series that followed, not only to the original

230) that the car should serve so superbly in this supremely civilized rôle and yet be capable of going off on the fire-breathing death-defying rampage as any real sports car once in a while should.

Let there be no doubt that the 230 SL could be and was a sports car. Any such doubts were allayed at the time of its introduction, when the Mercedes-Benz press relations chief Artur Keser took over a little circuit at Montroux, just over the French border from Geneva, where motoring journalists visiting the show could go and sample the car. It was a tight and tough little circuit only seven-tenths of a mile long yet comprising seven severe bends, all of them different and every one treated by Uhlonhaut, who was there to give demonstrations, as a means of proving that by the standards of the day the roadholding and handling of the new car were beyond criticism. As luck would have it there was another thoroughbred present there to provide a basis for comparison: Michael Parkes, son of the Managing Director of Alvis and responsible for much of the design and development of Ferraris, had visited the circuit in a 3-litre Ferrari 250GT Berlinetta. Parkes, let it be said, was a fine driver—anyone who could graduate as he did from a chain-drive Frazer-Nash to a Formula 1 Ferrari in the course of a decade must be good!— and in the mettlesome Italian V12 he managed to lap the testing circuit in 47·3 seconds. Uhlenhaut, who as we have seen was no slouch either, got down to a lap time of 47.5 seconds in the 230 SL.

How this industrial Pimpernel managed to go everywhere and achieve everything is still a matter for amazement. At that time he was in charge of a department numbering 880 people, among whom were 120 designers and 160 development engineers. Despite the scale of this oper-

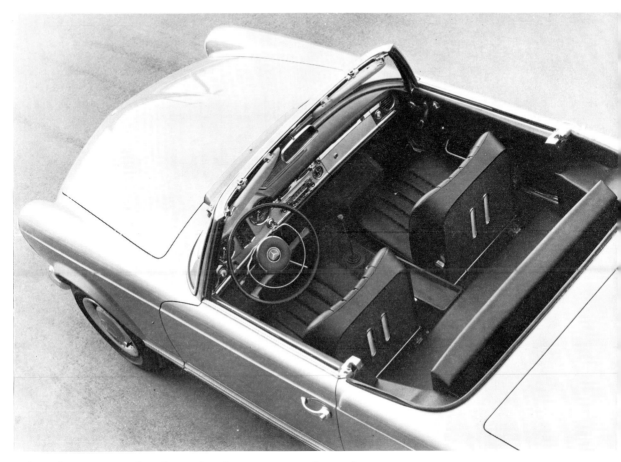

Lots of useful space behind the seats of the 250 SL

ation, he managed to keep in close personal touch with all development work, and by setting aside his evenings at home for the reading of technical reports, which can consume so much of an engineer's time, he contrived to pack thousands of miles into each year driving experimental vehicles so that he was always able to take—as he was always insistent on taking—the final decisions and the final responsibility in respect of car handling behaviour.

Those motoring journalists who were present all seemed amply convinced by the Montroux

This 280 SL had the soft top; too often, the 280 felt as though it had a soft centre

demonstration. The same theme came through all the reports: here, for some inadequately understood reason that might be geometrical but might equally be supernatural, was a car with swing-axle rear suspension which remained nevertheless a car which evidenced no treacherous tail-twitching oversteer but remained consistently stable in the understeering mode, a car which gave a gratifyingly resilient ride while yet torturing its tyres to limits that themselves seemed to be beyond reason.

If there were any who remained unconvinced, there was another demonstration before the year was out that carried a good deal of conviction with it. Driving a 230 SL, Germany's star rally man Eugen Böhringer and co-driver Kaiser won the Spa-Sofia-Liège Rally, the Marathon de la Route. What was more, they won it by a comfortable margin—and since that Marathon of the Road was recognized by all rally drivers as being the epitome of everything that was tough and trying, both for the car and for the crew, that success really meant something.

Organized by the Royal Motor Union of Liège, the Marathon was first run in 1931 over a 2800-mile (4500 km) route that passed from Liège through western Germany and Austria, the Dolomites, and over the Appennines to Rome, turning north to return to the start by way of the French Alps. Even in those early days it was run practically non-stop at an overall average speed of about 32 mph (50 km/h); but in the years after the World War, as cars grew better the event was made tougher, and the distance grew to 3200 miles (5150 km), taking in speed tests on such passes as the Stelvio in Italy and the Col du Galibier in France. As the going became harder and the speeds faster, the Austrians and Italians began to complain about this unbridled riot making mayhem on their roads, and for 1961 the event was re-routed to miss Rome and go down through Jugoslavia into Bulgaria. The year after Böhringer's victory in the 230 SL, when a BMC-entered Austin Healey 3000 won the event after failing to stay on the road while trying to stay in front of the Mercedes-Benz in 1963, even the Jugoslavs felt it necessary to call a halt, and the Marathon was demoted to become a tedious regularity event on the Nurburgring. As a road event, in the words of that accomplished crewman John Davenport, 'the Marathon may be dead but it will always be remembered as the toughest of them all: an event where to finish was an achievement in itself, and where the organizers were so confident that their course was a full test of man and machine that they allowed any modification at all to the car, and never had to resort to coefficients or driving tests to find the winner'. What modifications were made to the winning SL cannot be established; the probability is that they were fewer and less drastic than the modifications made to rival cars, but better executed. The main point was that the whole field had started with equal opportunities, and in the end Böhringer had beaten them all. Now who was to deny that the 230 SL could be a sports car?

But not, insisted the diehards still rut bound, when equipped with power steering and automatic transmission. Blinkered nit-wits that they were, they failed to understand the import of the acceleration figures that were published when the motoring journals began to test the car in both forms. Certainly the automatic version was slower in initial acceleration from standstill, when the fluid coupling was suffering maximum slip and maximum efficiency loss: from 0 to 50 mph (80 km/h) took 0·9 second longer in the automatic than with the do-it-yourself gearbox— but from 0 to 60 (97) took only 0·7 second longer and from 0 to 100 (160) only 0·5 second longer. In other words, from 50 mph to 100 (80 to 160 km/h), the speed range in which acceleration is most important when actually driving fast on the road as opposed to taking artificial and irrelevant performance figures on a test track, the automatic version actually accelerated faster! This was not because of any wondrous mechanical efficiency in the automatic transmission; of course, there was some power loss through the fluid coupling, which, even when operating at the top of its range and as near to lock-up point as it could get, still suffered

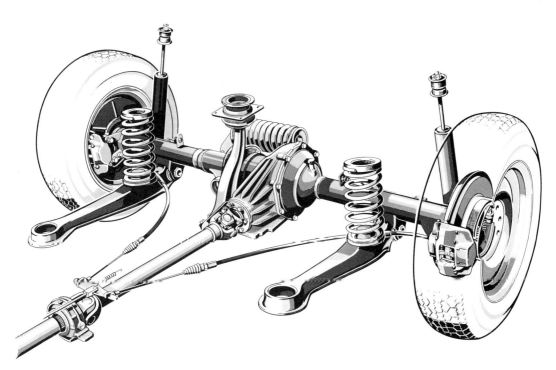

*The three major attachments
of the rear suspension to the
hull involved large rubbers*

two per cent slip and a like efficiency loss,
reflected (together with any further power losses
in the automatic gearbox) in a top speed deficiency of as much as 3 mph (5 km/h). It all
depends, though, what you mean by efficiency:
most of the power all of the time can be better than
all of the power some of the time, and what little
the automatic lost in its transmissive ability it
regained by not wasting time during gear
changes. Given an ordinary driver, a private
owner careful for his own property being the
obvious case, one employing neither the skill nor
the brutality of professional test drivers whose
snatched gear changes during acceleration testing offer roughly equal chances of snapping the
passenger's neck or sundering the drive line, the
manual version would be relatively slower still.

As for the power steering, the case is only

slightly more debatable. By reducing the effort needed at the wheel, the servo assistance made it possible for the steering to be quickened from 18 to 16:1, the effect of which was to reduce the number of turns of the steering wheel in going from lock to lock from $3\frac{1}{2}$ to 3. With such compact turning circles (less than 33 feet/10 m) between kerbs) this represented decidedly quick steering for a car that weighed more than 2900 pounds (1315 kg) at the kerb. With fuel and two passengers aboard, fifty-two per cent of the total weight could be borne by the rear wheels, but that still left a fair load for those touchy front tyres to take, and when they were hauling the nose of the Merc into a tight fast corner the reaction could certainly be felt at the wheel. It must be admitted that some of the feel was lost when the steering was given hydraulic assistance rather than hydraulic damping; but the loss was not critical, and the greater sensitivity possible through fingers that had to transmit less muscular effort at the steering wheel's rim probably made up for the deficiency.

It was a pity about the steering wheel, as it has been about almost every Mercedes-Benz steering wheel ever made. As something to hold onto it was fine: big, thick, and rigid, it would have been a worthy addition to any gymnasium. As a driving tool it was too big, typical of the grossness that so often infects whatever Daimler-Benz make. As something to look at, it was wholly repulsive— but even though it looked wrong, it was in the right place. The driving position was quite splendid, a relaxed and natural one that could be tailored to suit almost any physique and almost any taste aided by almost absurdly thick seats (the *Grosser* complex again!), which wrapped around the torso to lend lateral support in corners, while the cushioning swept up at the front to give support under the thighs — perhaps a little too much support for short-legged people constantly kicking at the clutch of the three-pedal version.

The constant kicking was due to the fact that the engine was tuned to give its power high up in the rev-range, with peak torque occurring only 1000 rpm below peak power. It was necessary to keep the machinery singing in a fairly high tessitura if the full potential performance of the car was to be realized; admittedly the flexibility associated with fuel injection was there, so that the engine could be made to pull from as little as 20 mph (32 km/h) in top gear if you cared more for your left leg than your main bearings. It just would not pull hard, being very lazy indeed until turning at 2500 rpm, and only really getting the bit between its teeth at 4000. High rates of crankshaft revolution are after all what allow a small engine to match the power of a larger but more sluggish one, and many a neophyte unfamiliar with the genre found the performance of the little Merc either disappointing or worrying, according to whether or not he allowed the engine to rev higher than he was accustomed to hearing an engine. It was difficult for such a newcomer to accept that the engine was safe and free-running right up to 6500 rpm, but once he learned to enjoy it the car would really go, cruising serenely at 100 mph (160 km/h) and 5000 rpm, and still with 500 untroubled rpm in hand when flat out at about 120 mph (193 km/h).

It was not to reduce cruising rpm that the engine was enlarged to 2496 cc from the time of the Geneva Show in March 1967. Ever since the new 2·5-litre 6-cylinder engine with seven main bearings was introduced for the 250 series of saloons at the Frankfurt Show in August 1965, it had seemed logical and inevitable that this engine

Aren't those seats superbly shaped? And isn't that wheel too big?

should replace the little 4-bearing 230 unit in the SL, and nobody was very surprised when it did so, involving a new type number.

The 250 SL had no more power (nor more piston area, for the increase in displacement was achieved by lengthening the stroke), but with the larger valves and ports in a redesigned cylinder head it breathed better to exploit the greater displacement and so yielded practically ten per cent more torque. Because the curves of torque and BMEP were flatter, power did not fall off so readily above the 5500 rpm peak, so the top speed rose by 3 mph (5 km/h) or so; more important was that the acceleration was a good deal brisker, or alternatively the car could be driven in a more relaxed fashion with less recourse to the lower reaches of the gearbox. Not that the gearbox was in itself unpleasant to use, for the baulk-ring synchromesh was quite effective and not unduly resistant; the trouble lay in the typically German choice of ratios, grotesquely wide so that, while top gear was a long lope, bottom gear was a nasty noise; the other two just had to be fitted in between so as to fill the gaps as well as possible. On the road this meant that if maximum performance were to be achieved there was very little choice but to scream the engine's head off in each gear before changing up, which was something that the average fat gentleman or expensively beautiful lady was not inclined to do. Even with the automatic transmission, which might be expected to do it for them, the performance was inhibited by clinging to the higher gears: if the selector lever be left in the fully automatic position (marked with a figure 4 on the quadrant) upward changes occur at lower speeds than if the lever is snicked back to position 3, which locks top gear out and enables the engine to be run up to maximum rpm in third. Flick the lever farther back to position 2 and third gear is locked out as well—and moreover the car will move away from rest in bottom gear, whereas in other circumstances it would start in second unless the accelerator pedal were thrust right down into the kick-down position, in which case there would be a nasty jerk as the transmission

*The 280 SL facia was just as flashy as the earlier cars';
and the wheel is too big*

switched to bottom gear and the car shot away. It was a sensible arrangement in catering for the requirements of the sporting drivers who would use the inhibitor lever freely on twisting roads, and the nylon-lined quadrant slot was so shaped as to make free use of that delicate wand-like gear lever easy and fool-proof, in a manner that other manufacturers have been inexplicably reluctant to copy. Doubtless their customers would not understand the purpose of the provision; doubtless a lot of Mercedes-Benz customers did not understand it either, for it was not long before the 250 engine was replaced by another even larger.

It was just long enough for some hot-headed people to make mistakes. One of these was the former racing driver Stirling Moss, held in at least as high esteem by Daimler-Benz (for whom he had driven masterfully in the 1955 racing team, most memorably winning the Mille Miglia) as by the populace at large. A great protagonist of Mercedes-Benz production cars, he had acquired a 250 SL, but when he heard that a 2·8-litre version of the engine had been developed he moved heaven and earth to get one, insisting that it be installed in his car. Quietly the company tried to dissuade him, explaining how difficult it would be, but he was adamant, and at vast inconvenience and scarcely less expense he had the work done privately, which involved prolonged wrestling matches with the exhaust system and a trouble-some series of ancillary transpositions. Barely was this work completed than Mercedes-Benz announced what they had hitherto had to keep secret—the 280 SL! Much of the engine was un-changed, an alteration to the distances between the cylinder bore centres allowing the bores to be enlarged by just under five percent and the power output to be increased by 10 bhp. Naturally the car was brisker than ever in acceleration, though lower final drive gearing (which made it livelier still) prevented the maximum speed from being any higher, the rev-counter needle reaching the red-line limit at 121 mph (195 km/h). That limit was still 6500 rpm; despite the much greater displacement, the new engine could sing as high a note as the old ones.

Motoring life is like that: as often as not, performance grows better though design may appear to grow worse. On paper these 7-bearing engines, the 250 and 280, were less elegant than the original 4-bearing 230 for they had wholly or alternately siamesed bores, shorter con-rods, torsionally more flexible crankshafts, and because of the additional main bearings (which were no greater in diameter than the original four) they needed much more complicated balancing, with ten counterweights hung on the throws instead of the three that had sufficed on the 230 engine. Nobody cared: the 280 was faster and more flexible. What probably mattered more to the customers was the eminently sensible and long overdue reduction in necessary maintenance, the hopelessly old-fashioned regreasing interval of 2000 miles (3200 km) in the 230 SL having been extended to 6000 (10,000), mainly by putting rubber where the grease used to go.

Alas, the car rather felt like it. Rubbery, that is—and generally rather more squashy and soggy than the little sports car that had been so impressive just a few years earlier. By 1968, when the 280 SL came on the scene, there was evidence of fatty degeneration of the heart. The car seemed to roll and lurch more in response to steering input, and by no means all of it was due to any increase in the servo assistance or decrease in the lateral assistance of the tyres, which were still the same size as before but were by now of fairly conventional radial (or near-radial, with a crown angle of 88°) ply tyres instead of those perilously stressed belted bias types. The suspension just seemed softer, less firmly anchored, less firmly damped, less firmly controllable. The car had grown heavier, too, by a couple of hundred pounds; the only consolation was in its acquisition of a better-balanced braking system with discs at all four wheels instead of only at the front ones. The braking response was no better, though, being still unexpectedly over-reactive at low speeds. If they were used frequently and hard

from high speeds, on the other hand, the pedal began to demand a good deal more effort—in other words they suffered mild fade.

It did not matter a great deal. People seldom drove the SL like that any more. If there had ever been a demand for the closer-ratio five-speed gearbox that was available to special order for the 250 SL, it must rapidly have faded. If you saw one of these cars on the open road, you would probably observe it to be driven as though it were

Under the bonnet of the 280 SL things have changed, such as the big brake servo and master cylinder in the foreground

murmuring down Bond Street. Apart from an isolated and rather unsuccessful quest for rallying honours by Dieter Glemser, no attempt was made by the factory to persuade customers of something in which they were no longer interested. Those with a good memory were still in no doubt about the 230 SL: but it was difficult to be sure about its successor at the end of the decade. Was the 280 SL a sports car?

S-class Luxury

It was on 21 June 1948 that affairs began to improve rapidly for Daimler-Benz AG. That was the date when currency reforms were introduced with an effect that was no less than startling, and the company was suddenly freed from the paralysis that had overtaken it at the end of the war. It meant hard work for them, but that seemed natural enough and within a year new cars were again being built. Within twenty years, the firm had delivered 2,000,000 of them, giving it a very special place among the élite half-dozen manufacturers who might justifiably claim to make the best cars in the world.

Yet what constitutes a good car? By 1968, with environmentalists and conservationists bellowing to each other like mastodons across the primeval swamps, a wave of anti-motoring sentiment was beginning to infect the world, and it was not difficult to detect a suggestion that the only good car was a recycled one. Since they could not afford to succumb to this popular movement, Daimler-Benz determined to survive it; but it made the early 1970s a time of frantic reappraisal and furious work, of fulsome moralizing and with fingers crossed. As social and legislative pres-

sures grew up to raise the standards of motoring safety, the company's engineers strove to stay well ahead of the game by concentrating not only on the mandatory secondary safety measures such as crash survival provisions, but also on primary safety so as to ensure thoroughly stable and predictable behaviour in emergency manoeuvres. Uhlenhaut might be due to retire soon, but nothing was going to undermine the Mercedes-Benz philosophy that, if anything could be preferable to surviving an accident, it was avoiding having an accident.

At the same time the Stuttgart engineers catered for what their customers might appreciate more with first-class automatic transmissions and power steering, high standards of body finish and furniture, and strictly maintained service networks for cars that were now far too complex for the uninitiated to work on with anything other than a cheque-book.

Late in 1972, the culmination of all this was to be seen in the new series of large cars, the Mercedes-Benz S class. At first glance it looked like a mere restyling job, albeit one that had been drawn with an uncharacteristically fluent hand; but closer inspection revealed it as a cogent attack on every objection that could have been raised against earlier cars made by Mercedes-Benz or indeed by anybody else. Diehards excepted, of course—and there are times when the earnest enthusiast for motoring finds it hard not to align himself with their rank. When cars grow heavier, thirstier, slower, more costly to buy and to maintain, more difficult to comprehend systematically, more difficult to admire aesthetically or to worship emotionally, then it is tempting to decry every novelty and every development on the grounds that motoring, like *Punch*, is not what it was—if only because, like *Punch*, it never has been.

Sports photographer Gerry Cranham invented the zoom-blur technique; by the time the 350 SL appeared, everybody was using it

59

*Styling studies for what was
to be the 350 SL*

Stylists drew and discussed for four years before arriving at the 350 SL shape

All these accusations could be levelled at the new generations of cars emerging from all quarters in the early 1970s, there being scarcely one that could not be decried on some grounds by some critic declaring himself a purist; in all sorts of ways, the cars were more refined than ever in the past, but the process of refinement was carrying them teetering to the brink of degeneracy.

Decadence is a fascinating process: like so many supposed vices it offers much that is attractive. It is even so in motoring: the trouble with all these modern monstrosities, corrupted by agitators and legislators to the point where one

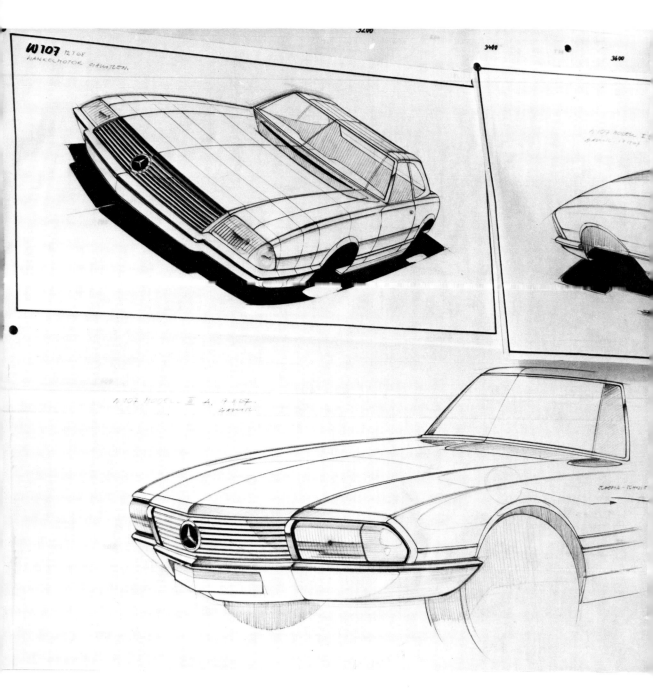

sometimes wonders whether the design engineers should not retire altogether and leave the job to the politicians, is that so often they are much nicer to drive, and very much nicer to be driven in, than their predecessors. This, thanks be to Mercedes-Benz Engineer-in-Chief Dr. Scheren-berg or whomever, was true of the S class. It was likewise true of the new generation of SL road-sters, conceptually (and to a great extent mechanically) the direct descendants of the old ones, but reflecting superficially the progress assumed in the new ones.

All the safety features made the new cars heavier than the old ones. The larger size made

Sketches for a proposed face-lift: 1967 below, 1968 above

Director Wilfert, responsible for Mercedes-Benz bodies, criticising a 350 SL mock-up

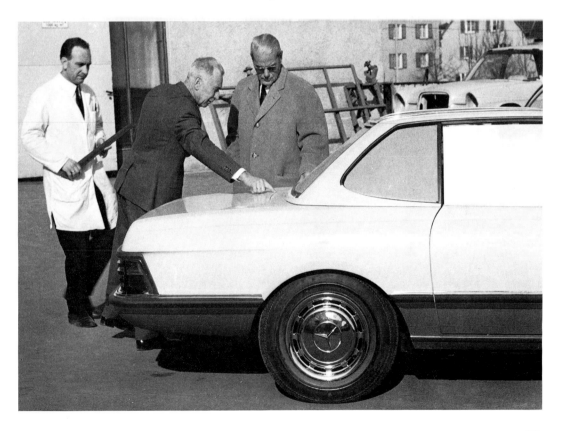

63

*A 350 SL styling prototype
which did not reach
production. Neither did the
C-111 beyond*

them even heavier still; but the bigger engines
offered fair compensation, so that the new SL did
everything the old one did and generally did it
rather better.

Apart from its objectives and the stylistic echo
of the coupé roof that could supplant the fabric
top (and was just as monstrously heavy to man-
handle as that of the earlier cars) the 350 SL had
very little in common with the earlier two-seaters.
The 3·5-litre V8 engine, with electronic fuel injection by Bosch, was the one that had earlier been
installed in the 280 SE 3·5 and 300 SEL 3·5 saloons,
a fine modern overhead-camshaft V8 that once
again had a placarded limit of 6500 rpm but gave

The SL series was always very popular in Britain, where this 230 was probably not called Elise

The characteristic kerbing rib can be seen on the tyres of the 250 SL, while the frontal view of the red 280 SL shows the earlier screenwiper pattern which gave such good double-handed coverage of the glass

350 SL and 450 SLC show by contrast the passenger-blinding wipers parked where they must surely be an aerodynamic nuisance too. The light-alloy wheels are costly options which nevertheless proved very popular

Simple sensible practical rally preparation, the sort that makes a car more useful rather than less, is evident in this view of one of the SLC entries for the South American rally

Above *This is a most sympathetic picture—even the colour of the gravel is right—but it shows how well the 15-inch wheels of 1986 grace the appearance of the SL*

Right *In 1971 few noticed, and those may have approved, but after fifteen years, during which the noses of most cars have been lowered, sloped, and generally wedged underneath the wind, the whaleback bulge of the SL bonnet is very noticeable—especially to the driver*

its peak 200 net installed bhp at 5800 and its peak 211 torque at 4000. With that sort of tractive effort available, one might expect the automatic gearbox to be a mere three-speeder. This was so in the case of the ordinary big 3·5-litre V8 saloons, in which the engine was matched to a converter coupling and three-speed automatic gearbox; the 350 SL was expected to be driven differently, however, or was considered at 3400 lb (1542 kg) to be a mere lightweight, so it had the older style four-speed transmission and simple fluid coupling, the important thing about which is that the torque output always equals the torque input. In other words you use the control lever as you

Final high-speed test of the 350 SL at the Hockenheim track before the car went into production

73

If flashier outside, the 350 SL at least had a less eye-offending facia

might the gear lever of the three-pedal car, the only difference being that on most roads you will use more fuel and get better results. That is not a bad piece of trading, except that a fifteen-mile-per-gallon (18·8 litres per 100 km) rate of consumption does not allow you to go very far on a tankful before you find yourself down to the last two gallons (nine litres) or so. Treat the old 230 SL gently and it would give better than twenty-five mpg. . . .

In fact it was the 350 SL that one learned to treat gently, because for all the refinement of its new S-class suspension it could be a bit of a rogue. At the rear the wheels were carried on the ends of semi-trailing arms slung from a hefty sub-frame, the effect being to reduce camber changes to half of what they were with the old low-pivot swing-axles. On the other hand there was a devil of a lot more tractive effort going through those tyres, which admittedly were much more modern but lamentably not much more generous in size.

Moreover, the front suspension was so splendid that the car's attitude became quite sensitive to abrupt changes in acceleration or braking in mid-corner. Lift off smartly when halfway round and in a twinkling you would be all the way round, and as like as not facing in the opposite direction. The effect can be disconcerting in the wet, for some of the various makes of tyres which found their way on to these cars in pursuance of the Daimler-Benz multiple sourcing policy behaved on wet roads like well-greased eels. Others were better, but if you felt tempted to explore their capabilities you would soon learn to appreciate the power-assisted steering, now standard and now very much better, more communicative of changes in feel, than most other cars' systems. Of course, the steering wheel was still far too big, but what did you expect? And the wheelbase was

Dimensionally very similar to the 230 SL, the 350 SL would nevertheless have looked taller and narrower without those horizontal ribs and grooves: the illusion of length makes a car look lower

just a couple of inches longer than that of the 230 SL, and the track an inch or so less and the turning circle about the same, but for all the servo aids that huge tiller had now to be twirled $3\frac{1}{3}$ turns to get from one extreme of lock to the other. In the 1970s there could be nothing wrong with that: you did not think this a sports car, did you?

Perish the thought and the expression! In that decade, no regular solid citizen would care to be thought of as the owner and driver of a sports car: it had anti-social overtones that would do no good at all even to the most beautifully expensive lady. No, the SL was now a high-speed luxury tourer, and the fact that it was a mere two-seater (with even more space behind the seats than in the past, though possibly less in the luggage boot) should be recognized as implying nothing to do with the car itself but only a more widespread employment either of contraceptives or of boarding schools.

Popularly grouped with the S-class cars, the 1971 350 SL appeared before them and did not have their elaborations of suspension

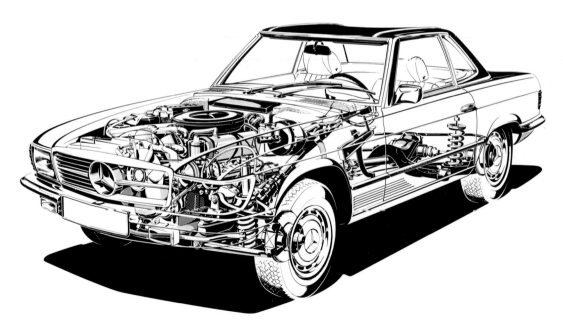

As is frequently the case with the former and invariably so with the latter, that was not the end of the story. It so happened that Daimler-Benz had a newer and more promising engine in their armoury, and just to demonstrate what we were saying earlier about the benisons of decadence, we had to thank the American emissions regulations for it. The plain fact was that by the time all the necessary de-toxing and smog-abating paraphernalia was plumbed into the 3·5-litre V8 engine's alimentary tract, the thing was simply not powerful enough to give the big heavy S-class Mercedes-Benz the sort of performance that was expected of it in the American market. At this stage in the history of automobile degradation, the new 'smog' regulations were at least self-negating if not positively counter-productive; it being impossible while complying with them to improve the engine's metabolism, the only cure for a gutless wonder was to give it a bigger belly.

Washers and wipers for the 350 SL headlamps

*The automatic transmission
selector was one of the very
best—and the wheel was* still
too big

*It was a beautiful interior,
though, even with gaitered
lever and four pedals to suit
the synchromesh
transmission and parking
brake*

Accordingly Daimler-Benz readied a 4·5-litre V8, which, with all the mandatory stifling for the Land of the Free, succeeded in developing just about as much net power as the 3·5-litre. All they had to do in the spring of 1973 was to jettison all those onerous trappings and they had an S-class 450 with a lusty 225 bhp at the driver's disposal.

Actually there was a good bit more to it than that, a very good bit: with the bigger V8 came a new kind of rear suspension, a geometrician's paradise that kept the car stable under power, resisting tail squat, and helped to keep it stable under braking by abetting the frontal anti-dive

Heavy and bulky, the overhead-cam 350 V8 engine felt much lustier than the 280 six. Money torques?

geometry. It was this as much as anything that prompted the international jurors for the European Car of the Year Award (and Setright was one of them) to vote the 450 SEL the Trophy. It was still possible to make the throttle do some of the steering for you when cornering energetically, but there was none of the hypersensitivity that marked the 350 SL: hit the throttle or the brakes in mid-corner and the 450 SL would change its course, but not dramatically, and a vague hint at the steering wheel (yes, it was still too big), a suggestion of movement with one finger rather than a brutish and insensate heave, was enough to keep the car pointing where you wish.

Tell it not in Gath, publish it not in the streets of Askelon, but there were certain individuals who on the quiet liked to treat the 450 SL as a sports car. One of them, a very certain individual indeed, did it professionally: big and dark Erich Waxenberger from the Experimental Department, who joined Daimler-Benz about the time when Fangio was being fitted for his Grand Prix driving seats, had assumed the mantle cast off by Uhlenhaut who, when the 450 appeared in 1973,

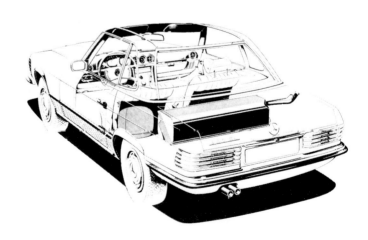

A drawing issued to show off the car's safety features, for example impact breakaway mirror, non-slip steering wheel and well protected fuel tank

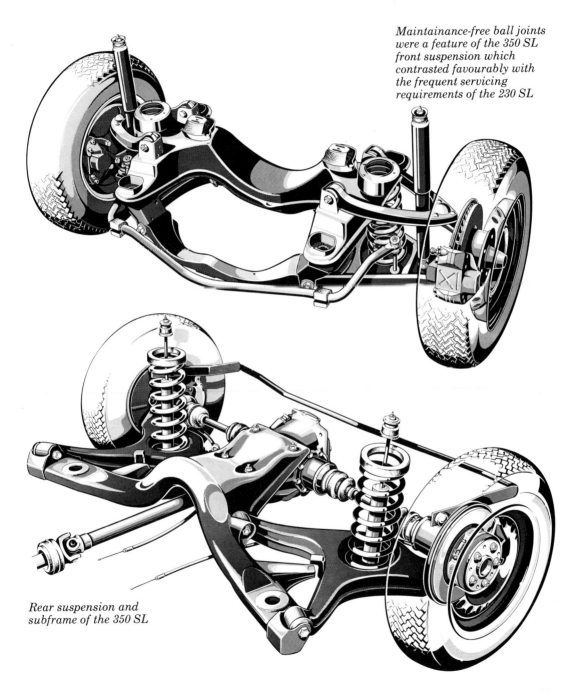

Maintainance-free ball joints were a feature of the 350 SL front suspension which contrasted favourably with the frequent servicing requirements of the 230 SL

Rear suspension and subframe of the 350 SL

was a retired gentleman with an outstanding reputation and a large yacht.

Driven by Waxl, the 450 SL is a car that can do 135 mph and feels as though it is doing it sideways. He was a virtuoso, and he knew it, and every time he demonstrated a Merc the passenger was left in no doubt that Waxl could do the most outrageous things and that the car would survive them. It was after all part of his job to see that it could, and part of his qualifications to be able to find out. Spending a lot of his time hammering around the test track inside the factory grounds, or testing on the Nurburgring, or tearing off to the Italian Alps for some week-end skiing, he was the epitome of the hard-driving engineer who really knows his car and what it can do.

The customers could only benefit by this development work. When he found some cause for dissatisfaction, Daimler-Benz honour had to be satisfied; and this demanded that not only Master

The 280, 350, and 450 SLs were pretty much the same externally. The hardtop did not have the style of the earlier concave beauty

When the turbocharged diesel version of the C-111 Mercedes-Benz went on a record-breaking spree, a fine gathering of Daimler-Benz technocrats was photographed with the car. From left to right they begin with Joachim Kaden and Hans Werner; then, in sunglasses, is Erich Waxenberger, head of the experimental department and a prodigious driver. On the other side of the car stands Dr Hans Liebold, and next to him is Guido Moch, in charge of the test department and the most superb driver of the lot. Then there are ranked Karl Heinz Göschel, Kurt Obländer, Professor Doctor Hans Scherenberg (who is in charge as Technical Director of Mercedes-Benz) and Friedrich van Winsen

The 450 SL may not have looked different from the 350 SL, but was a much better car—even the American version (there is a tiny 'unleaded fuel only' notice above the filler hatch) which suffered a slight loss of power compared with the less regulation-inhibited European car

Slidecatcher Waxenberger could drive the car hard without running out of road, but also that an ordinary customer (if somebody with that much money to spend on a car can be deemed ordinary) could do it too.

Much of it can be done within the grounds of the factory, where an astonishing variety of handling tests and suspension tortures has been packed into a fairly compact area: high-speed straights, assorted corners, stretches of bumps and ripples and punishing pavé, troughs of water and circles of varied stick-and-slip materials on which to try steering and skidding. There is a water trough deep and long enough to worry a 40-ton artic, a battery of huge air-screws that can generate a side-wind like a tornado. Most surrealistic among all these artificial realities are the two banked corners, which enable high speeds

to be maintained despite the compact extent of the proving grounds; one is ordinary enough and not terribly steep, treated by Waxl as an ordinary corner, slinging the SL through it at the tyre-whining limit of adhesion (0·83g on Michelin XWX tyres, said he) with the tail hanging out and front wheels held on a little opposite lock to catch the drift. For him that was an ordinary corner; but on the other banking he was just as likely to remove his hands from the steering wheel and leave the car to find its own way. This banking is vertical at the top, a giddy half-bowl of a corner through which the car can be driven at its maximum speed while the driver is rammed down into the seat by centrifugal force, the blood draining from his head and his belly feeling as though he had eaten a five-course meal in one gulp.

Although I was abnormally conscious of the

USA legislation to protect domestic lamp-makers and insurance companies doomed cars for the North American market to quadruple headlamps and extended bumpers

The 450 V8 engine can be summed up as remarkable in nothing and impressive in everything

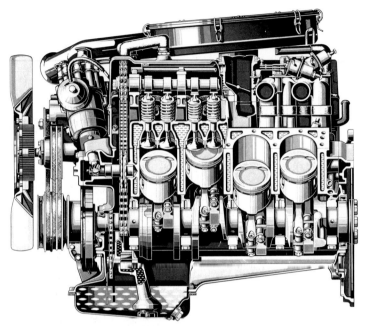

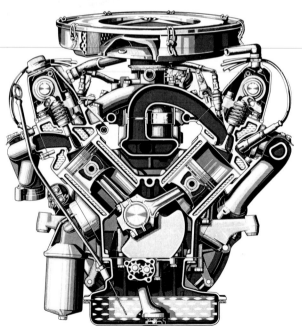

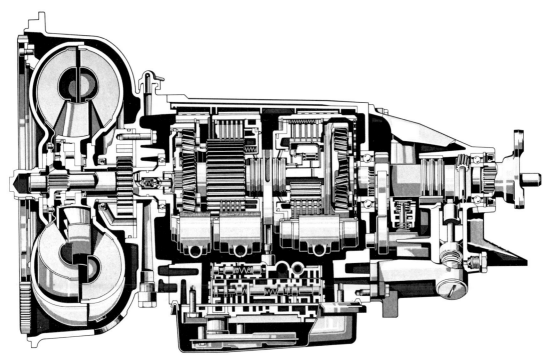

weightiness of matter when I tried it, the Stutt-gart theory is that what this treatment does to the driver is immaterial. More important is what it does to the car, for the static weight of the solidly built 450 SL was magnified two and a half times by the centrifugal loadings, so that the tyres and suspension bore an unforgiving 4·3 tons as it sped round the banking. If they could not take it as a matter of course every couple of minutes as another lap was reeled off, the whole lot would go back to the drawing board. Even more cunning was the technique Waxl showed me for making the suspension crash through to its bump stops on one side only, accompanied by a brief take-off and landing in mid-corner! It is a left-hander set in a section of the course that allows plenty of room for any ensuing accident, and the road is raised and lowered twice in a mathematically precise double ripple. Hit these humps at just the right

Always thorough, Daimler-Benz put a secondary oil pump in their automatic transmission so that the 450 could be towed, making it surely the first car designed to be reliable even in the broken-down state

speed (a matter of calculation rather than of experiment) and the suspension is caught in sympathetic vibration. The treatment the car gets at this place is anything but sympathetic.

If, as I did, you felt like having a fling, the SL could be flung. For a 4·5-litre V8-engined luxury roadster weighing more than a ton and a half even when empty, it was absurdly agile. No hard work was entailed: the power-assisted steering wheel was something to caress, the big pedals likewise, and the magic wand that gave unrivalled control over the superb automatic transmission (three-speeder at last, with a splendid converter coupling that smoothed almost every change into an insensible slur) responded to a few ounces of fingor proosuro. Only the acccleiatui pedal remained to remind you that in four inches of movement lay 225 horsepower. Here at last was an SL that was even more fun than the 230.

Slightly Longer Coupé

'Power corrupts', said Adlai Stevenson in emulation of Lord Acton, 'lack of power corrupts absolutely.' Accordingly there may be some who consider that the ultimate expression of the Mercedes-Benz S class was in 1975 to be found in the 450 SEL 6·9 saloon, which had more engine, more brakes, more suspension and indeed more of most things than any other car in the range. Given the first item in that list, it needed the remainder; but they did not necessarily make it a better car than its rival as the best of the bunch, the 450 SLC.

The C stood for coupé, which is ridiculous. Coupé means cut short, which is just what this car was not: instead it was an SL that had been stretched to make room for four adult occupants. It would make better sense if the word were Comfort.

It was indeed the most comfortable of them all. The saloons were roomier, but their expansive seats, dimensioned and contoured to cosset the bottoms of the tycoonly stout, offered less intimate support to the torso than did the superbly shaped seats of this sumptuous car, which was itself superbly shaped. Gorgeous though it looked from outside, the SLC was most

The fenestration and slats gave a better view outwards than inwards

especially delightful within: those seats were surely among the best anywhere, for I once spent twenty-four out of twenty-six hours literally on end in one, sitting at the wheel and never suffering the faintest twinge of discomfort. The seat might not fold back all the way, but it went far enough to constitute an adequate bed if sleeping were the object, and might accordingly thus qualify the SLC as a sports car. Other qualifications manifested themselves in due course. . . .

The SLC was surely never intended as a sports car. It was so elegant, so superbly balanced in line and form, so exquisitely contoured to look beautiful from any viewpoint, that to subject it to the gross indignities of any kind of track, be it in a

Some US customers were really thorough, compounding the futilities of federal requirements with dreadful wheels and tyres

*Daimler-Benz have never
made a production car more
beautiful than the SLC; few
others have, either*

*The ribbed rear lamps stay
clean even in foul weather*

racing arena or a rallying forest, would be sheer vandalism. And yet the car begged to be driven in a sporting way, positively solicited the fast corner, the fine balancing of foot and hand, of centripetal and centrifugal accelerations. It was surely the best balanced and most impeccably behaved Mercedes-Benz yet to have been built for common sale. Maybe it was a trifle less agile than the shorter and lighter 450 SL, the initials of which subscript became meaningful again; but in consistency and progressiveness of response to all control inputs, especially through the steering and brakes, it was the two-seater's superior— which was just as well, because it looked it.

It might be improvident to rely on looks, unless you looked closely enough to read the small print (no, not very small—modesty is not a failing commonly encountered either in Stuttgart or in its satellite showrooms) on the ravishing rump of this beauty. What looked like a 450 SLC might turn out to be only a 280 SLC, which was not as good; or indeed it might be a 350 SLC, which was not as good as the 280.

More people bought the 350 version than either of the others. The 280 was not widely marketed, in fact, having been intended as a sop to those customers who had no wish either to pay the taxes or to suffer the opprobrium associated with large-capacity cars in certain countries where their like was, in the aftermath of the 1973 fuel crisis, deemed immoral. To this end Daimler-Benz gave it as a nasal implant the new 6-cylinder twin overhead-camshaft 2·8-litre engine that they had originally introduced early in 1972 to invigorate four new Mercedes S-class models based on existing 'new generation' hull structures. It was the arbitrary fiscal structures of Europe that determined the engine displacement, and their recent experience in the design and development

The SLC wheel was still too big; on the other hand, the brake pedal was now big enough for use by either foot, as a good automatic deserves

SLC interiors were tweedy, and more comfortable than they looked

of V8 engines that prompted them to revert to that most attractive of configurations, the in-line six, to meet their new purposes. Given a crankshaft of sufficient torsional rigidity, a straight six is as nearly vibrationless as an engine can be: there may in fact be an unbalanced sixth-order tremor. Nothing with fewer cylinders can be as good, nothing with more will be any better until you have so many that you can make two straight sixes—by no means an impossible prospect for a firm that once ruled the world of motor racing with a two-stage supercharged V12.

Why did they bother when they already had a 6-cylinder 2·8-litre engine? The single-camshaft 2778 cc machinery found under the bonnets of 280 S and SE Mercs held little promise of adequate power for their future purposes, whereas a twin-camshaft engine would. Moreover the latter was likely to ease the problems of exhaust emission control. God Bless America.

This new engine, then, was virtually new

SLC bodies on the line at Sindelfingen

throughout, in construction if not in concepts. Seven main bearings it had, and a counterweight on every one of the twelve crankshaft webs, and an elaborate new twin-mass torsional damper to cure the Achilles' heel of the in-line six. With all sorts of other refinements, including high-pressure fuel injection, transistorized ignition (with a built-in 6500 rpm cut-out and 50,000 miles/ 80,000 km imperturbability) and a compression

Coupés are mixed with saloons on the three final assembly lines

Coupé and S-class hulls in transit through the body factory, at a rate of 6000 a month

One day, Mercedes-Benz would learn to park their wipers away; passengers in earlier right-hand-drive Mercs found them very obstructive

ratio high enough for high power and low enough for low-lead fuels, the outcome was 185 net bhp, and that is why the 280 was a nicer car than the 350. The latter had only fifteen horsepower more, was burdened by more frontal weight, had a gearbox with more widely spaced ratios, which was therefore less pleasant to use, and did not make such a nice noise.

None of the three made much noise anyway, but the most restful was obviously the slower revving 450 SLC, for although its overall gearing was the same as in the 350 it had so much more torque that

less resort to the lower gears was necessary. Even with all the tractive effort that the bigger of the V8s could impart to those cunningly suspended rear wheels, the 450 SLC was not all that fast. It was after all a heavy car, so its acceleration was not all that much better than that of the SEL saloon. Even had it been slower, it would not have mattered, for it was still the nicest of all the cars and particularly easy to drive as fast as it would go because the gearchange points programmed into the automatic transmission were so optimized that there was nothing to be gained by

Smaller-engined SLCs were just as fetching as the 450 appeared, even this 350 . . .

using the control lever to inhibit the automata. Using it during the approach to a corner was a different matter: as with all other current and recent automatic Mercs, the most encouraging stability and the most lively responses are secured by using the control lever as freely as the rev-counter's message will allow. Even so, the performance of the 450 SLC should not be overrated: among its contemporaries, a Jaguar XJ-S or a Bristol 411 could out-perform it, but that ignorant neighbour of yours would not be as impressed as by the SLC, which really did look fast.

It drank fast too, and at thirteen or fourteen mpg (20·2 litres per 100 km) its average speed across country would be lowered by the need to refuel every 250 miles (400 km) or so. It was not as though one needed the stop for a stretch of the

. . . and especially the 280 with this lovely twin-overhead-camshaft six-cylinder engine

The 280 engine was also available in the SL

legs: as already mentioned, one could remain comfortable in the SLC for twenty-four hours at a stretch, and in that time one could, but for the necessary restoration of fluid balances, go a very long way. On that particular occasion I did not seek to: the object was to see what this fast car was like when driven slowly. The answer was that it felt the same at any speed as at any other, which must surely entitle it to rank as a rare triumph of engineering. There are so many fast cars that are only nice when driven fast, and too many slow cars that are frightening when you try to drive them faster. The S-class Mercedes-Benz did everything well, as a matter of course, and none did everything better than the SLC.

Top left *Wool-tufted 280 SL ready for wind-tunnel testing*

Bottom left *Another kind of airflow visualization is by smoke in the wind tunnel. The subternasal spoiler here was a prototype for the 450 SLC 5.0*

Above *Final version of the bib graces the lightweight 450 SLC 5.0*

107

The lightweight 5-litre version of the SLC bore the final version of the bib together with a tail spoiler

As a matter of course, it could be made a *voiture de course*. With very little modification (by the standards of the sport) a 450 SLC was rallied quite successfully in Britain for a couple of seasons in the middle 1970s, and then in the early austral spring of August and September 1978 four 450 SLCs were entered in the South America Rally, and one of them won it.

108

The Vuelta a la America Sud, as the rally was officially called, was staged by the Argentine Automobile Club, starting and finishing in Buenos Aires and travelling through all ten countries of the South American continent, a matter of 18,500 miles (30,000 km). Of these, 3700 (6000) were to be covered at racing speeds, and some of the route involved Andean passes (almost impassable, it was forecast) climbing higher than 15,000 feet (4500 m).

The rules did not allow engine tuning or improvements to the transmission or body, so the competing cars (prepared in Stuttgart together with three 280 E models) were substantially standard production models adapted for the poor road conditions and the unusually realistic regulations. All were equipped with a duralumin undershield to protect the engine and transmission, and with bump and rebound stops for the front and rear suspensions. Special equipment included bucket seats for the driver and co-driver (the back seats were removed), a roll-cage, a special container for tools and accessories behind the seats, a 120-litre (26·4 Imp. gall, 31·7 US gall) fuel tank, a two-way intercom system, navigating equipment, a special jack and two spare wheels, which were shod rather curiously with 195SR14 M+S Dunlop tyres. Then there was the safety equipment, including oxygen respirators (15,000 feet can be distressingly high), a big fire extinguisher, a well-stocked medical kit and some distress signals. In effect the standard was for Group 1 Touring Cars, and out of eighty teams from Europe, Africa and the Americas it was the 450 SLC of the British pair, Andrew Cowan and Colin Malkin, that won.

It would have been nice to see a 450 SLC do well at Le Mans too, in the 24-hour sports car race which took place a couple of months earlier in

The spoiler on the tail of the 5-litre SLC would probably have been bigger if Germany's regulations were less restrictive

that year. One was present, as fully tuned as possible, as expansively tyred and faired as feasible. It looked marvellous, and was impressively stable through the twistier parts of the circuit, but its overall lap speed was just not high enough for it to qualify for participation in the race.

Several SLC racing appearances were made in or about 1978, mostly by a car which had been prepared by AMG. This tuning firm had started in 1967 as a partnership (one of the proprietors was a former Daimler-Benz employee) working in an old country millhouse; with a dozen years of experience and growth behind it, AMG could now derive quite a lot of power from a D-B engine, and do quite a lot to improve the handling and road-holding of a Mercedes-Benz chassis. Their SLC often acquitted itself respectably, but motor racing had long departed from its earlier traditions of roadworthy cars being raced; in the new, brash, heavily commercialized and irrelevantly obsessional activity that sport had become, the SLC looked out of place—even though it scarcely looked like an SLC. What should have been a thing of beauty had been made a beastly brawler.

By that time Daimler-Benz had in any case taken their own steps to make the SLC a truly fast car. Just as it had actually been the first Mercedes-Benz to carry the 450 engine, so in September 1977 it became the first to bring to market the new light-alloy 500. Great things were afoot: great sums of money were being spent to make the S-class saloons lighter, so that they could achieve better fuel-consumption figures. The cars would thus appear less anti-social to the poor people who could never afford them and would happily use the 1973 oil crisis as an excuse to deprive the rich of them. Just to show how commercial and insincere the whole business was, the new V8 engines slated for the revised 1979 saloons would be made almost wholly of aluminium— which demands so much energy (in the form of electricity) to make it that all the fuel savings of years to come would scarcely compensate for the initial expenditure. . . .

The public would never recognize the paradox. The public would praise D-B for this new expression of social conscience and technical competence. Just to be sure that the public would be right, a couple of years' service experience with the new engine in the old SLC would be an effective small-scale test.

A couple of days driving through the Black Forest, down to Konstanz and back to Stuttgart, served me well as a small-scale test. Finding it at the airport was not difficult: just as a peek at the posterior of earlier SLCs served to spot the 450,

Lighter by a couple of hundred pounds and lustier by a couple of dozen bhp, the 450 SLC 5.0 at last went as well as the SLC should always have gone

a full-span rump-reading now revealed the figures '5·0' added to the 450 SLC code. Even for the illiterate, there was a modest spoiler ridging the top of the boot lid, a little thing but enough to identify this as the 450 SLC which went as well as the 450 SLC always ought to have gone. This, then, was the car in which—in blissful legality on the public highway, and in perfect and tactful safety among all manner of other people going

Little bits of wood veneer presumably confirmed that the '5.0' was still a gentleman's *sporting coupé*

*D-B claimed that lightweight
construction in aluminium
alloys would help to save
energy (by reducing fuel
consumption); but they
avoided mentioning that
aluminium takes much more
energy to produce it than does
iron*

about their daily drives—I averaged 133 mph over 20 miles, 126 over 40 miles. I could find cars in which to do it faster today, but not so easily in the 1970s; and of the few which were as fast as this, and as fast as this looked, hardly three could display such good pedigrees by not feeling as fast as they actually were.

How fast was it? The makers claimed 0 to 100 km/h in 8·5 seconds, but mine was slower. They claimed a top speed of 140 mph, but mine went faster. By my Heuer chronograph, the car with two adults aboard reached 100 km/h in 8·6 seconds, 100 mph in a further 9·6, and ten seconds later it was doing 122 mph. Magnificently high-geared so that (despising the vulgarities of drag-strip criteria imported from the USA) it could haul itself up to 66 mph in bottom gear at its redlined 5800 engine rpm; it could reach 108 in second gear. In top (the SLC did not have the four-speed transmission destined for the saloons) the same rpm would have corresponded to 158 mph, clearly beyond reach; but my car registered 137 mph, just past the 5000 rpm peak of the power curve, going uphill, and 149 downhill. One had to be content with cruising at only half that speed, however, in order to cover 320 miles (it sounds more significant in metric terms) without resort to the reserve petrol supply.

That meant 18·9 mpg, not good but not what *hoi polloi* would call really bad. Was this a proper return for the expense of an engine claimed to weigh 88 lb less than its precursor? Compared with the iron-engined 450 SLC, the 5-litre version weighed only 253 lb less—a mere 7·6 per cent of the 3338 lb standing on those fairly fat Michelins, and unlikely to have much effect on the performance. The aerodynamic bib and tucker probably helped a little, though their principal contribution was to high-speed stability; and the higher

gearing, raised by 12·5 per cent in the final drive, would by itself only make the car slower. No, the thing that made such gearing possible and everything else justifiable was the thing which gave 240 bhp at 5000 rpm, not mention 298 lb/ft at 3200, and was made—like the bonnet, the boot lid, the bumpers, and old Adam himself—of the dust of the earth. In this case, that meant aluminium.

It was aluminium alloyed in a special way, developed by Reynolds for similar use by Chevrolet and Porsche. A low-pressure chill-casting procedure for the block was followed by electrolytic etching of the bores, removing the surface of the aluminium matrix to expose the unusually large silicon crystals so generously distributed in it. On these exposed crystals rode the rings and iron-plated pistons, without any intervening cylinder liners, and without any of the problems of differential thermal expansion which iron liners present.

Eliminating the liners was the secret of light-weight engine construction, and enabled the bores to be enlarged so that although the overall dimensions remained those of the old iron 450, the piston area and displacement were increased by 10 per cent. This was well matched by increases in power of 10·6 per cent, in torque of 12·2 per cent, and in exhaust port area by 11 per cent—this last by intriguing valves 2 mm larger in head diameter but 2 mm more slender in the stem, and sodium-filled in a rare return to ideas that had prompted Sam Heron, half a century earlier, to invent this internal cooling for the valves of the Wright Simoon aero-engine.

Communication between the valves and their cams was now through finger followers sitting on zero-lash hydraulic fulcra; but really all such details, and they were exceedingly numerous, might be dismissed. The inescapable and quick

The new alloy block revealed the necessarily greater attention given to stiffening

Alloy components (and larger bore-holes!) reduced engine weight by about 88 lb (40 kg)

117

Far left *Timo Makinen in the South America Rally*

Left *Makinen again, but not quite the same car: a new front wing, and a lot of patching*

Above *Makinen rolled his SLC! Here are the roadside repairers already at work*

conclusion was that this was plainly a good engine, one of the most encouraging that a driver might find anywhere near his right foot; and it was just right for the lovely and deserving SLC.

It usually went unheard, for there was plenty of sound-deadening material (something had to account for all that weight), and the high gearing further reduced the noise at any given speed. Should you not fancy the speed given, however, a kick of the throttle pedal or a flick of the transmission lever goaded the most gorgeous growl from somewhere deep in the tiger bay, and the car seemed to leap—except that a leap is soon over, whereas this went on and on, a great surge seeming to tip the road down the car's gullet and turn the horizon bluer, as though a contracting universe were the essence of some new Daimler-Benz cosmology.

Sadly, it was the SLC itself which was to perform the disappearing trick. When that alloy engine came of age in 1979, accompanied by a similar but smaller version of 3·8 litres replacing the old 350, the new S-class saloons (for which they had all along been destined) were revealed to be so much cleaner aerodynamically, so much lighter structurally and in detail, so much more road-worthy in their suspension and running gear, so much faster and more refined and more economical and more of everything that can be expected to go with being more expensive . . . so much more up-to-date, in short, that the ageing SL cars began to look positively crude. It was already eight years since they had been reskinned over the basic structure of the pagoda-roofed paragon of eight years earlier still.

The development chief, Professor Werner Breitschwert, and engineering chief Friedrich van Winsen, together had done marvels in giving expression to policy decisions that had been

taken in 1972, before the oil crisis. The character
and opulence of Mercedes-Benz cars had to be pre-
served, the modernity and practicality and efficiency of them had to be drastically improved;
and in the process it was inevitable that the road-
sters would be left behind. For the stubby SL,
grown increasingly butch with the passing years,
there might be a marketing niche for a long time
to come; but the SLC, in representing the S class
in coupé form whereas saloon-based coupés had
previously lent glamour to otherwise stolid series,
was no longer a match for the refinement of the
1979 saloons.

*Tony Fowkes driving a 450
SLC in the 1977 Tour of
Eppynt rally*

In September 1981, two new 'dedicated' coupés labelled 380 and 500 SEC took over. They were as heavy as the saloons to which they corresponded, and their styling suggested an unhealthy preoccupation with American muscle-cars of the 1960s; but the preoccupation was more with wealth than with health, for the prime markets for these costly coupés were expected to be the USA and the Arabian states of the Middle East. Neither there nor in the domestic German market did rigour and reticence go as familiars: the luscious SEC was calculated to succeed, and the lean SLC was doomed to succumb.

The Salzburgring race was the AMG car's second 1978 appearance, and it finished second. On those huge Goodyear racing tyres it cornered very impressively

123

Still Lingering

Those new SEC coupés were only part of a most important package of developments which, at the end of 1981, invested the S class with enhanced appeal. If those upper-class saloons were to perform properly their crucial role (which was, bluntly, to lead Daimler-Benz into an assured and profitable future), they had to be better adapted to an environment which had shown itself able to change with frightening rapidity. They had to be made competent to deal with any rise in standards in any direction, be it economy, primary or secondary safety, reliability, durability, or any of the other abilities by which the fickle public may judge its cars.

At that time, although the 1973 oil crisis had been betrayed by a glut of oil in succeeding years and was by now known to have been an entirely artificial and politically fomented 'crisis', it was still fashionable to be concerned with energy conservation. Thus the late-1981 marketing 'package' was entitled the 1982 Energy Concept; but while real improvements had been made in fuel economy (at vast expense in manufacturing energy), the new versions of the S-class saloons were replete with such developments as would also make them go faster, steer better, stop more safely, and cosset more luxuriously. Considering

an annual research and development budget more
than ten times greater than the real cost of racing
in those impressive but distant Uhlenhaut days,
anything less would scarcely be forgiveable.

In the case of the SL, to expect anything similar
would have been unreasonable. There were limits
to what could be done with the old chassis, and

*From the departure of the
SLC until the arrival of the
1986 face-lift, the roadster
range—280, 380, 500—had
settled down to look like this*

125

Face-lift might be a misnomer for what came in 1986: the lower jaw appeared to have dropped. The new and deeper subternasal dam reduced aerodynamic lift over the front of the car by 30 per cent; had it not, fashion would have insisted that it did

those limits were fast being approached. The 380 and 500 engines had already been slotted in, once production of them had reached full swing in 1980, but most examples were apparently bought for their looks. It was understandable: though they might look considerably less svelte than the very early SL roadsters, there was now nothing else which looked remotely like them at all, nothing which so successfully conjured up all the desired imagery of the expensively beautiful and the idly rich. Better still, provided that two strong men could be found to lift off the absurdly heavy roof, the car could be driven in open form the better to display its lines and, most important of all, its driver. Emphatically not now a sports car, it had become (in the biological sense, if in no other) a sport car.

The performance was not significantly affected, could not be significantly affected, by the changes wrought in the 1982 Energy Concept. The 380 V8 was slimmed in bore and stretched in stroke; both V8s were given higher compression ratios and all manner of electronic circuitry with which to integrate the workings of ignition and injection systems, including fuel cut-off on the overrun and air-blast atomization at the injector nozzles during idling. It was all very clever, and it worked: although the power curves had lower peaks, the areas under the curves were much greater, as overall improvements in volumetric efficiency bore witness to wholesale revision of inlet and exhaust tracts and combustion chamber shapes. More to the immediate point, fuel consumption was usefully reduced.

Not that people cared much. By this time, it was clear that oil was abundant, and fuel was not expensive. The cars were, and that was what mattered: people had to *know* that they were expensive, to know that their drivers must be rich, and therefore successful—which, by this time, was in most societies the main criterion of what might loosely be called virtue. Whatever their virtues, expensively beautiful women still adored the SL.

They still do. It has just been revised again, and probably for the last time, in 1986. The 500 engine survives almost unchanged, but improved breathing (aided by bigger inlet valves and a new cam profile) has brought its bhp up to 245, nevertheless a long way short of the 300 available from the new 560 engine now being installed in a few of the big saloons.

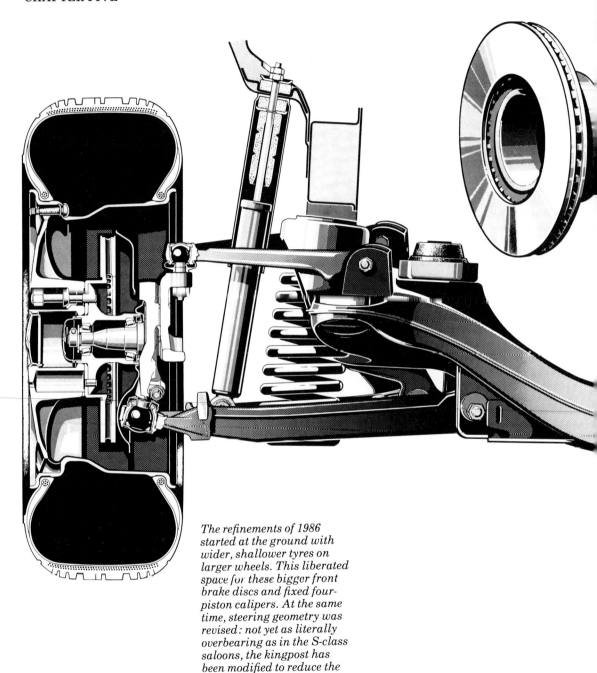

The refinements of 1986 started at the ground with wider, shallower tyres on larger wheels. This liberated space for these bigger front brake discs and fixed four-piston calipers. At the same time, steering geometry was revised: not yet as literally overbearing as in the S-class saloons, the kingpost has been modified to reduce the scrub radius or offset

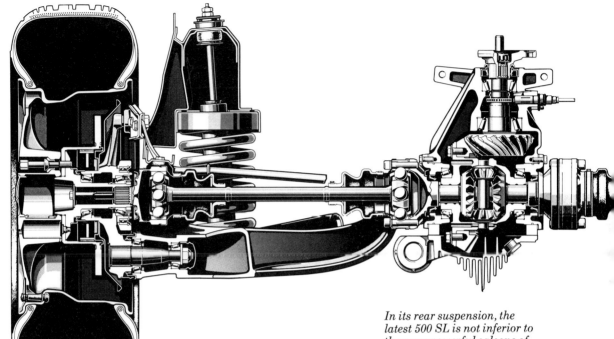

In its rear suspension, the latest 500 SL is not inferior to the more powerful saloons of the S class. The swivel at the bottom of the hub-carrier, and the extra linkage at the top to control it, combine to resist tail-squat when accelerating briskly from rest. Other refinements evident in this drawing are the costly ball-spline universal joints and the final-drive housing which proves that D-B draughtsmen can switch planes without leaving their seats

As for the 380, that has by way of bigger bores become a 420, the more easily to procure improvements in power and torque to 218 bhp and 243 lb/ft respectively. Here too the bigger valves and expanded inlet system of the 500 have been echoed, and with updated electronics incorporating microprocessor interpretation of operating conditions, both engines are evidence of Daimler-Benz determination to make their products more modern than they look.

To be consistent with this policy, the old 280 had to go. It went; in its place is a 3-litre in-line six, first seen in the 300 E saloon which crowned the W124 series of mid-range saloons when they made their debut in December 1984. Except for

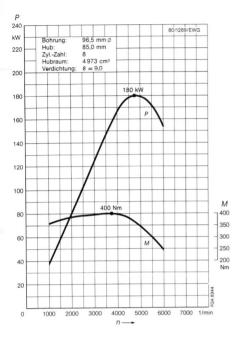

*The power output of the latest
500 engine equals 245 bhp
DIN, an improvement on the
231 of the previous version.
Even with exhaust catalysis,
with which Germany and
therefore all Europe were
threatened by the Liberal/
'Green' campaign of 1984–85,
it still gives 223 bhp*

carrying its weight rather high, it is an elegant engine, with crossflow breathing through opposed inclined valves operated by a single overhead-camshaft. Although the zero-lash adjusters keep the valve gear quiet right up to the 6200 rpm maximum, the engine is intended to deliver plenty of torque at low speeds: seven main bearings may even more readily be taken for granted than the electronically stabilized idling and Lambda-mapped injection which constantly adjusts mixture strength according to all relevant circumstances. It is just a shame, though hardly a surprise, that the 300 SL it propels weighs 375 lb more than the five-seater 300 E saloon. . . .

If the two effective seats in the SL were truly comfortable and roomy, the contrast might be less painful. Alas, the sheer thickness of the seat structures, the need to mount them high enough for all the wiring and sound-deadening and adjusters beneath them, and the intrusive curve of the soft-top cowling behind them, combine to make the car now very cramped indeed for a tall person, though someone shorter could doubtless be comfortable no matter how stout. Removing the roof would make life easier and the view better, but it is very heavy and impossible to stow.

Even so, the car might still be so pleasant to drive as to justify all this. The engine and transmission (the latter now with a performance/economy selector switch to determine the mode and even the mood of gearchanges) are truly delightful, after all. The steering, heavier than the servo aid would suggest, is beautifully accurate and completely damped, improved perhaps by the new geometry accompanying a long-overdue adoption of front suspension rather like that of the S-class saloons. Further improvements in response come from tyres of lower profile than ever before on an SL, 205/65VR15 tyres on newly

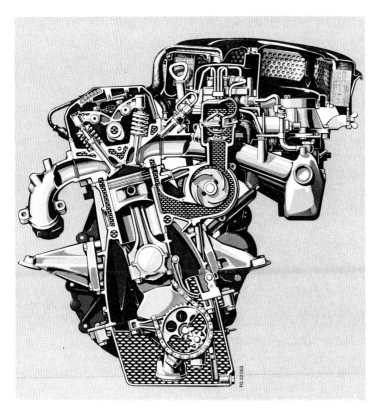

Likely to be most popular in the 1986 range is this engine, which enables the car to be designated 300 SL! It is an engine which carries its heaviest masses (crankshaft, head, etc.) rather high, for reasons valid in the W124 from which it comes. In the hefty SL, the effect escapes notice

enlarged wheels. They would increase the stability of the car in yaw; but something horrid has been done to decrease its stability in pitch. Open the throttle and the already high nose rears up before you as though to reassure American drivers that this car has all the muscle they remember from their own cherished horrors of the 1960s. Open the throttle on a damp road and something quite different happens: the rear wheels spin wildly, betrayed by the geometry of their motions so that the tyres cannot find traction. It is all a frightful pity.

One wonderful new attribute allays the fright. Standard on all three versions of the SL is that automatic system for preventing excess braking power from locking any wheel: ABS (*Anti-Blockierung* or Anti-lock Brake System) ensures that the car will safely stop, in a straight line and as quickly as possible, even in circumstances where the driver has little control over making it go. And just as well: the car exhibits such awesome solidity that, far from fearing for one's own safety in an accident, one dreads the thought of how much destruction it might wreak wherever it struck.

Never mind. All this coming and going and stopping, so long a feature of SL history, will take on an entirely new guise in a very few years, perhaps as early as 1988 or as late as 1990. Daimler-Benz are well advanced with their work on a truly advanced car (coupé, or even sports car, should not sufficiently describe it) that will cost a substantial fortune to buy and demand real justification for the privilege of driving. It promises to be as outstanding in its times as the original gullwing 300 SL was, and it may be as passionately and uncritically coveted as the pagoda-top 230 SL, and every one of its successors, has been. It will be preceded by saloon-based coupés which, like the present SEC series, will satisfy most of the 'cosmetic' market: production and sales of the 230 CE and 300 CE coupés, derived from the W124 series, are due to commence in the spring of 1987.

Then, when the new supercar (which may also be coded SL) has arrived, the old SL—now by far the most antiquated chassis on the firm's stocks, and yet the most glamorous car of them all—may be suffered to depart. Until then, it is too early to turn hindsight upon it; all we can fairly do is to note that an adoring public has never, in more than a quarter of a century, allowed it to be taken out of production. Ever since the Mercédès name lost its accents, the letters SL have provided its most memorable suffix.

Airflow over the roadsters being what it is, it is hard to imagine the tail spoiler on the 500 SL being anything but a status symbol. The new frontal dam is functional, though, and helps to identify the 1986 pattern. Most apparent, and a very effective improvement both functionally and visually, are the larger-diameter road wheels bearing lower-profiled tyres

Index

Acknowledgements

Without the help of Daimler-Benz AG in Stuttgart, Mercedes-Benz (United Kingdom) Limited and Mercedes-Benz of North America Inc, and the Mercedes-Benz Club Ltd this book would have been without a wide cross-section of illustrative material. Many others also helped fill in the gaps. They are, in alphabetical order: *CAR* magazine, *Car and Driver* magazine, Bob Constanduros, Continental Tyre and Rubber Company Limited, Cornfield Carriage Company of Eastbourne (owners of the 250 SL and 280 SL shot in colour), Peter George (owner of the red 230 SL), Reinhard Klein, London Art Technical Limited, Jean-François Marchet collection, Carrozzeria Pininfarina (Michael Frostick collection) and Bill Quinn of *Road Test* magazine.
Nicky Wright took many photographs especially for this book, most of them under uniquely adverse weather conditions.

6